The Story of 12 Platoon, Dog Company, 1st Battalion The Duke of Wellington's Regiment

Korea 1952-1953

These poems are an extract from *Memories and Imagination*, Volume III: 'The Bloody Hook'
The fictionalised memoirs of

John Hollands MC

THE WAR POEMS OF A YOUNG SOLDIER

Here's a story of war, as ancient as primitive man,
A yarn rooted in the days when greed first began.
It has a fresh location, and a new generation involved,
But still the same slaughter with very little solved.

First published 2010
First Reprint June 2010
2nd Reprint August 2010

Edward Gaskell publishers
Old Sawmill
Grange Road
Bideford
Devon EX39 4AS

isbn: 978-1-906769-09-3

THE WAR POEMS OF A YOUNG SOLDIER

Typeset, printed and bound by
Lazarus Press
Caddsdown Business Park
Bideford
Devon
EX39 3DX
www.lazaruspress.com

This book is dedicated to all the young national
servicemen who were dragooned into
fighting in Korea and sacrificed their
lives for the sake of others who
they never knew, or ever
would have known.

Acknowledgements

I would like to thank the following
people for assisting in various ways:
Trevor Hunt, David Chapman-Andrews,
Christopher Price, Ken Fisher,
and Lesley Pyne.

Contents

Introduction

The war poems you are about to read are an integral part of my fictionalised memoirs entitled *Memory and Imagination*. Volume III of these memoirs, *The Bloody Hook*, deals with my experiences as a national serviceman, as seen through the eyes of my alter ego, or literary clone, Sajit Contractor. This book is fiction. It is not historically accurate. As the title implies, it is based on memory, embroidered by imagination. Regimental histories give the facts; novels and poetry tell you what it was like in human terms.

The poems are attributed to Private Rupert Sandwitch who features in *The Bloody Hook*. We were very close friends. We joined the army together at Catterick Camp and the friendship ended twenty months later on a hill in Korea known as The Hook. We were part of 12 Platoon, Dog Company, 1st Battalion The Duke of Wellington's Regiment. I was the platoon commander and Rupert was our wireless operator (88-set). Neither of us was suited to military service and our friendship was based on a shared interest in literature. Rupert lived for poetry. He used rhyming couplets in everyday conversation and in Korea he extended this quirk to writing short verses which he pinned on our platoon notice boards. They kept morale high. Their irreverence convinced men that they were having their say, that Rupert spoke for them all. They often upset our OC, Major 'Earl' Gray. He had enough sense not to ban them, but every now and then he would charge Rupert with insolence.

Rupert Sandwitch died the day after the third and final Battle of The Hook on May 28th/29th 1953. His death was the result of a leg wound. Whilst he was in an American MASH unit, I took a party of volunteers back on to The Hook to dig out the wounded and dead from blown-in bunkers and tunnels. This enabled me to salvage the poems Rupert had written during the preceding months. They were in his kitbag in what was left of the platoon command post, but Chinese satchel charges had damaged and burnt them so badly that they were in tatters, many unreadable. Sorting them out into something readable (which I did on the troopship returning from Korea) was like trying to reconstruct fragments of an ancient and crumbling manuscript. I still have my original copies of the poems.

You will form your own opinions as to their merits. I was too close to Rupert to make an objective judgement. All I will say is that they give an accurate and echoing picture of our life in Korea. They form a chronological picture, not just snippets plucked out at random, as is so often the case with war poetry. They also reveal a young man who matured rapidly on experiencing some of the harshest conditions ever known in warfare. His poems show little resemblance to the still fashionable Great War classics of men like Owen, Graves, Blunden, Sassoon, and West. Rupert would not have had it otherwise. Those Great War poems he admired he could recite verbatim, but otherwise he shared W. B. Yeats's view that too many of their poems were 'all blood, dirt, and sucked sugar stick' .

Rupert often shows inconsistencies in his attitude to the war and this should not cause surprise: as a nineteen year-old he was still forming his opinions. Sometimes he demands to know why we were expected to face death, yet at other times he displays remarkable sang-froid. He had no early links with the Duke's, and certainly no Yorkshire connections, but he soon became obsessed by the regiment and found Yorkshire men (or 'Eh by gums' as he called them) great characters. Most of all, he became obsessed by Tommy Atkins (who *was* a Duke).

The confusion among national servicemen as to why they were fighting in Korea was very understandable. They were not fighting for their own country but for the United Nations, a new and untried organisation. They were helping to uphold a thoroughly corrupt regime which was guilty of frequent and foul atrocities. Moreover, the Korean government was continually calling for the withdrawal of British Forces. They regarded the British government as Marxist fellow-travellers on account of the numerous protests we made about their atrocities. In truth, British troops only stayed in Korea in deference to our American allies. Furthermore, during the Duke's time in Korea the war had ceased to be a matter of repelling aggression. The UN had already achieved that. Our entire time was spent fighting in North Korean territory.

Rupert was a firm believer in poetic clarity. He rejected T. S. Eliot's contempt for excessive lucidity, and even the least gifted of his comrades had no difficulty in understanding his poems. Initially, Rupert assumed he would survive the war. His optimism sprang from his belief that he was preordained to become a poet. He had been awarded an Exhibition at Balliol College, Oxford, and he visualised a long academic career, dedicated to furthering the popularity of poetry.

With a few exceptions, Rupert's poems stand as he wrote them. Only out of necessity have I filled in gaps or missing/indecipherable words, and what is certain is that Rupert did very little revision on them. He didn't have time. Before each poem I have added brief notes (in italics) in order to set the scene and explain the conditions under which Rupert wrote. They also aim to give a sense of continuity and cohesion to our year in Korea. The whole story, from the day Rupert and I joined up at Catterick to the day I returned alone to Southampton, can be found in *The Bloody Hook*.

John Hollands

Rupert Sandwitch makes frequent references to Tommy Atkins, so it's not surprising that he wrote a poem about him and his famous last words. These last words came when Private Thomas Atkins died of multiple wounds in Flanders during the war of The First Coalition, 1794-95. At that time he had served in the 33rd of Foot (later to become The Duke of Wellington's Regiment) for twenty years.

Old Nosey (his Colonel, and later The Duke of Wellington), never forgot Atkins's last words and when he became he Prime Minister he decreed that the name Tommy Atkins should be used to typify all British troops, and this duly came about.

Tommy Atkins

Out of the eternal snows of the Hindu Kush
And the blistering heat of the Mysore bush,
Was spawned the spirit of the old Thirty-Third
And a humble private, famed for his final word.

Atkins was a veteran serving in his twentieth year
And in that time he'd got no higher than grenadier,
An illiterate giant but the regiment's best man at arms;
A Tyke who inspired others to fight without qualms.

It was in a Flanders field that he eventually fell,
With the Thirty-Third's rout not far short of hell.
Twice he'd been shot, and sabre-slashed galore,
With lethal wounds numbering close on a score.

Yet when he was found and removed to the rear
He alone was quiet, resigned, and devoid of fear.
All around him comrades moaned and cried out,
Men racked by pain, panic, and harrowing doubt.

Then up rode Old Nosey, splashing through mud,
And seeing Atkins lying there, soaked in blood,
Asked how he kept calm while others went berserk.
'Nowt to it, sir,' said Atkins. 'All in a day's work.'

Early Days at Catterick

Rupert Sandwitch joined the Royal Corps of Signals at Catterick straight from school. We underwent basic training together but were parted when I was transferred to the Potential Leaders Wing to try for a commission. Throughout his basic training, Rupert was forever in trouble. It got so bad that he and several other hard cases (including Animal Evans, Fletcher, Harry Winston, and Bertie Mee) were transferred to the Yorkshire Infantry Brigade at Strensel. There, they did basic training all over again. They got into further trouble when they threw an assault course competition. This resulted in them being posted to the Duke of Wellington's Regiment which was about to leave for Korea. It was then that I was reunited with them. By coincidence I had been commissioned into the Duke's and we all ended up in 12 Platoon.

Rupert's poems about his basic training and his posting to The Duke's were written whilst on the Troopship Devonshire, en route to Korea.

Basic Training

Bugles blared, echoing from a remote Asian shore,
And news broke of nations stampeding back to war.
I took note, but even with national service beckoning
Chances of involvement never entered my reckoning.

My call-up papers came and to the army I departed.
Basic training at Catterick, but I'm not downhearted.
Square bashing and bullshit the order of the day,
But I'm young and eager and at least there's pay.

Shining dull brasses with NCOs bawling,
Sleeping in lectures with officers drawling.
Arms drill! Fire drill! Dawn inspections!
A sadistic MO, blunt-needled injections.

Left turn! Right turn! At the double!
CO's orders for too much stubble.
Pressing trousers and blancoing gaiters.
Food's inedible, with black-eyed 'taters.

Sweaty bodies and blistered feet.
Excused boots: now there's a treat!
But no luck for me, although my blister's a beauty,
The MO, the bastard, prescribes 'medicine and duty'.

"Bloody this!" and "Bloody that!"
"Shut your gob!" "No bloody chat!"
"Salute it!" "Paint it!" "Stand by your bed!"
Pointless bullshit we soon come to dread.

Winter comes and Catterick instantly freezes.
No shelter from the biting northerly breezes.
So each night to the garrison cinema we retreat.
Not for the flicks, but warmth at a tanner a seat.

Tedious routines make the months drag out.
Naafi buns sustain us and we're all on snout.
Map reading, field craft, endless weapon training;
An assault course race thrown without straining.

They treat us as though we're guilty of treason,
With punishments beyond all rhyme or reason.
Jankers all round and we're inspected hourly;
'No leave for you lot,' our officer says sourly.

But we cock them a snook and laugh in their faces,
Certain we'll soon be basking in sun-soaked places.
But we're too cocky by far and soon rue our boasting,
They have the last laugh: you should see our posting!

The Duke's

Footsloggers we are now, my boys!
Doomed to crawl on our bellies.
Proudly we march under new colours,
Part of the Duke of Welly's.

Duke's, Duke's, we are now, my boys,
Bloody and heroic is our story.
Tommy Atkins was one of us, my boys,
So ours to enhance his glory.

To West Riding we're sent, without dissent,
To a fine county inspired by traditions.
Yorkshire men all, sturdy and tall,
Born and bred into fighting conditions.

Duke's, Duke's, we are now my boys,
Bloody and heroic is our story
Tommy Atkins was one of us, my boys
So ours to enhance his glory.

Halifax is our base. God, what a place!
With barracks like an old prison.
It's a town of flat caps, bombed-out gaps,
And tarts who're hardly a vision.

Duke's, Duke's. . .

In alleys they lurk, half-hidden in murk,
Each one poised like a painted vulture.
Hooked by their gall the lads screw them all,
And become addicted to Halifax culture.

Duke's, Duke's ...

Then the inevitable comes, the War Office (the bums!)
Hit us with an embarkation order.
So days on the moors, and the comfort of whores,
Give way to a Commie marauder.

Duke's, Duke's. . .

For Korea we're bound, where nothing is found
But death and horrific mutilations.
Where civil strife rules, we are the poor fools
Who'll fight as the United Nations.

Duke's, Duke's. . .

At Soton we debus with a minimum of fuss,
Voices raised in songs raucous and bawdy.
Bunting is flying and relatives are crying,
With the trooper resplendent and gaudy.

Duke's, Duke's. . .

A parting at sea is a new one on me
And fresh thoughts of death are distressing,
But why give a damn, fool that I am,
Hasn't the Padre just given us his blessing?

Dukes, Dukes, we are now, my boys.
Bloody and heroic is our story.
Tommy Atkins was one of us, my boys,
So ours to enhance his glory.

It was whilst on the Devonshire that the regimental band was disbanded and the bandsmen (all trained as stretcher-bearers, but nothing else) were transferred to 12 platoon, bringing us up to full strength. At the same time, the regiment's most celebrated old rogue - who no one knew what to do with - was awarded three stripes and made our platoon sergeant. This was Sergeant Darwin, known throughout the battalion as 'Old Origins'.

Once a week I gathered the platoon together and we entertained ourselves in the hope of creating esprit de corps. With so many young bandsmen, we had plenty of musical turns and Old Origins was a dab hand at playing the spoons. Rupert contributed unflattering verses about various characters in the platoon. These were short and light-hearted, in the vein of Stanley Holloway monologues. They always got a rousing reception, but alas only two of them survived.

Sergeant Darwin

Old Origins is short and grizzled
With a face that is made to match:
It's gnarled and battered and weathered,
His hair the texture of old thatch.
Beady eyes dimmed by the desert sun,
And hearing that's not much better,
Handicapped by half an ear he lost
Fighting with tribesmen in Quetta.
Rows of medals adorn his chest
Giving proof of campaigns galore,
And he often tells of a dose he once got
Monkeying around with a whore.
He's served his time in the glasshouse,
Been up and down the ranks a few times,

But he loves to add some distortions,
Giving spice and glamour to his crimes.
In Korea he will be in his element
Realising it's the last lap of his story,
And he won't give a damn what happens,
So long as we're all covered in glory.

Private Fletcher

In every platoon there's always a goon,
A hard-case who craves attention.
It is old Fletch with us
Who without any fuss
Has already done years in detention.

Fletcher's from Bow, as we very well know,
But his accent has traces of Hackney.
He is a sex maniac too
And without a good screw,
His whole body bursts forth in acne.

His catalogue of crime goes back a long time
And he lacks the backbone to rough it.
His treatment on the square
Struck him as bloody unfair,
So he sloped-off, telling them to stuff it!

And so he's regressed, as he's often confessed,
From serious crimes to mere triviality,
But his offences include
Everything that's crude,
With deflowering virgins his speciality.

We often maintain old Fletch is insane,
A man we'd be foolish to trust,
'Cos when bullets are flying
And brave men are dying,
We won't see Fletcher for dust.

Other than these weekly meetings, I had little social contact with Rupert and the others whilst on the Devonshire. Fraternization between officers and Other Ranks was not encouraged. Officers had luxury cabins whilst the Other Ranks sweated it out in hammocks below decks. However, Rupert's view of the journey to Korea would suggest that he found it interesting, even if not always enjoyable.

The Voyage Out East

For those who lack the will to wander
And whose spirit is sadly inert,
The sight of the sea and points yonder,
May well their outlook convert.

Away we go, me muckers,
The whole wide world to see.
Many a sight we'll gawp at,
But not for a tourist fee.

For many of the lads it was just such a case.
First Gibraltar, lonesome and mighty,
Then into the Med, dolphins leaping with grace,
And in Cyprus the call of Aphrodite.

Away we go, me muckers,
The whole wide world to see.
Many a sight we'll gawp at,
But not for a tourist fee.

Port Said was exposed as the bowels of the earth
With a repugnant smell straight from hell,
And the flotilla of bumboats jostling at our berth
Dipped and ducked in time with our swell.

Away we go, me muckers,
The whole wide world to see.
Many a sight we'll gawp at,
But not for a tourist fee.

So majestically we sailed from port to port:
Imperial forts with a tortuous past
Where many a Tommy invaded and fought
And jolly Jack Tar bled at the mast.

Away we go, me muckers,
The whole wide world to see.
Many a sight we'll gawp at
But not for a tourist fee.

Colombo, Singapore, and finally Hong Kong,
Each one sporting the old bamboo.
Girls lithesome and slinky in sari and sarong,
Gloriously sexy, but strictly taboo.

Away we go, me muckers,
The whole wide world to see.
Many a sight we'll gawp at,
But not for a tourist fee.

Finally we docked between Pusan's rotting piers
And beheld a country so obviously at war;
But bravado prevailed and we set off amid cheers,
To satanic hills steeped in blood and gore.

Away we went, me muckers,
Half the wide world we saw.
Many a sight impressed us,
But none prepared us for war.

<u>Into Battle</u>

Initially, Rupert was not impressed by either Korea or the Koreans. He found the people ugly, surly, and complacent about their country. The refugee problem was evident everywhere and he couldn't stand the foul smell of the countryside, caused by the hand-spreading of human waste in the paddy fields. Our journey north by train took several days, with frequent and unexplained delays, and this enabled us to get a good insight into the country. It wasn't until he got to know our house-boy, Kim, and several porters seconded to our platoon, that Rupert warmed to them.

The Koreans

They see their country as one of beauty and charm:
Part of the legend, 'The Land of the Morning Calm'.
They eulogize about serenity, with deep valleys kissed
And blessed by the damp swirl of a reoccurring mist,
And mountain ranges that change from green to grey
As they merge into a shimmering haze, far, far, away.
They boast of terraced hills where paddies spread,
And sparkling water tumbling over a pebble bed,
Rivers which twist and turn and rampage and roar
Through pancake plains towards the rugged shore.

We foreigners see things in a more pragmatic light:
A country laid to waste and a truly pathetic sight.
In Pusan there was nothing but filth and squalor,
With teenage girls selling themselves for a dollar.
And blighted refugees flocking in on a daily train,

Carriages bursting, risks bordering on the insane.
Men protruding from windows, clinging on by their nails,
Elders on the roofs, white robes billowing forth like sails.
A train of perdition, with death a constant bed-fellow
With many frozen rigid, gossamer skin parched yellow.
Survivors alighting in an avalanche, dense and teeming,
Forever struggling, fighting, pushing, always screaming,
Straight into the arms of the sadistic police from Seoul;
Licensed thugs who beat them on the pretext of control.
Bruised and dejected they cringe, tears smarting their eyes,
Realising that their cherished hopes were all based on lies.

Nearer the battle zone, the locals struggled with dismay,
Their farms studded by shell-holes in war's normal way:
And with every able man conscripted and made to fight,
The women and children worked alone, no help in sight.
Too frail to flee, and in dread of being caught in battle,
Their sole desire was to preserve their crops and cattle;
And as they toiled, they prayed to be left alone by everyone,
Especially politicians and cruel bastards flourishing a gun.

The General's Tool was written after our first pay parade in Korea. It dawned on Rupert how grotesque it was that he was being paid peanuts for fighting a war. National service privates got a pound a week, less barrack room damages! When the Company 2 i/c offered Rupert 19s 8d he saluted sloppily and remarked in his usual conversational tone:

"My goodness, Sir!
I'm amazed by how much Her Majesty can afford.
Especially when it includes full bed and board."

He was placed on a charge and fined two weeks' pay.

<u>*The General's Tool*</u>

We Tommies are paid but a pittance,
And we're never required to think,
Especially up at the sharp end:
Up there, blind obedience or sink.
But it's a pretty safe bet (with the idiots we get!)
That our orders up front will be suicidal.
Yet still we must obey, without any say,
Or be charged with being plain bloody idle.

Oh Tommy, you're only a laggard!
Oh Tommy, you're such a poor young fool.
Don't ever think for yourself, me lad,
You're nowt but a general's tool.

We Tommies have fought in the jungles,
Against guerrillas and swamps and all.
We've also fought in the mountains,
From the Alps to the heights of Nepal.
In deserts we've always been victorious,
With Kitchener and dear old Monty supreme,
And we fought the mad Mahdi without question
Though when we saw 'em we didn't 'alf scream.

Oh Tommy, you're only a laggard!
Oh Tommy, you're such a poor young fool.
Don't ever think for yourself, me lad.
You're nowt but a general's tool.

We Tommies have also known invasions,
And stormed across fortified beaches,
To say nothing of scaling sheer cliffs
Where we clung on to nowt like leeches.
But whatever the tricks we resort to,
And regardless of the press's ballyhoo,
When we hold out a paw, we get a quid (no more)
And then march off to our next Waterloo.

Oh Tommy, you're only a laggard!
Oh Tommy, you're such a poor young fool.
Don't ever think for yourself, me lad,
You're nowt but a general's tool.

The three stripes which Old Origins so unexpectedly acquired rather went to his head. Overnight, he went from being the battalion's great rogue to its fiercest disciplinarian, yet somehow it never worked. It would have with most rookies, but with the likes of Rupert, Fletcher, Harry Winston, Animal Evans, and Bertie Mee, he was wasting his time.

Old Origins' Tirades

Old Origins loves to subject us to a vitriolic tirade,
Especially when we are bolshy or idle on parade.
After ranting on about the failings of modern youth,
He treats us to his version of the plain bloody truth.

"Squaddies aren't what they were when I was young!
You lot are nowt but bleeding fairies, all highly strung.
You want pandering and comforts: no dirt or slime,
Else you moan and groan and bitch the whole time."

"You're lavished with cold, wet-weather boots
And weekly supplies of foul-smelling cheroots.
You even get free deodorants to squirt up your arses
Which you soak up by the gallon on R and R passes."

"Unless doused regularly by mobile showers
You wilt and wither, like delicate wee flowers,
And if you don't get your full quota of sleep
You poor little darlings collapse, all of a heap."

Then he quotes old dictums, supposedly consequential,
As though each pearl of wisdom is militarily essential:

"An army with fleas
Is soon on its knees."
Or

"If you stick-up your head
You're bloody soon dead."
Or

"An army in retreat
Soon has sore feet."
Or

"Beware a dead Chink,
He don't half stink!"
Or

"A blob on your knob
Will delay demob."

After each proclamation there is a pregnant pause,
As if Old Origins is expecting a round of applause.
Then off he stalks, muttering to himself with pride,
Chuffed to bollocks at having given us a rough ride.

We disperse, seeing it as another platoon joke.
How else can you react to such an old soak?

One of Rupert's shorter poems came after we had spent two days improving the defences on the reserve defence line: Kansas. Our area of responsibility was Gloucester Hill, where an heroic stand was made by the British 29th Brigade during the Battle of the Imjin River in 1951. Many remnants of the battle were littered about, or buried just beneath the surface.

Gloucester Hill

Now all is done: desolate, silent, and sanctified.
Rifles piled in peace, the last bayonet long struck.
Sacrificial blood caked, dried, and gone to earth,
And the hum of decaying flesh long nullified.

Trenches crumbled, and rusty guns that no longer fire,
The cordite signature coursed off in a wayward wind.
Hills bald and dusting, trees dead and skeleton bare,
Barren acres waiting for time and nature to re-attire.

Now, the Imjin no longer twists and turns, tinted red,
And a Cross to Curtis stands where the Chinese fled. *

** Lieutenant Philip Kenneth Edward Curtis, of the Duke of Cornwall's Light Infantry, (attached to the Gloucestershire Regiment) routed a large Chinese machine gun post single-handed, for which he was awarded a posthumous Victoria Cross.*

As we marched off to the front line, the music of our buglers attracted the locals. One of them was a young orphan boy named Kim. He attached himself to us and wouldn't be shaken off. Eventually, he became our houseboy. When we heard the details of his flight from the north, we realised just how evil the communist regimes were. Ironically, when the Armistice was signed, Kim chose to return to his home in the north, which only serves to emphasise the last line of 'The Koreans' . We watched with sadness as he waded across the Samichon to join the Chinese. We never heard any more of him.

Kim

When the Chinese first attacked and the
Yalu River was crossed
The forward positions of the United Nations
Were irretrievably lost.

Terror gripped the locals, and those in the
Path of the advance
Took to the road with alacrity, seizing
A desperate chance.

UN officers fled in panic, their cowardice
Precipitating a shameful rout;
And as they drove off in tanked-up transport,
Their sole cry was, 'Bug Out!'

With their troops so callously abandoned,
And left to a foul fate,
The roads were soon grid-locked with
Anarchy in full spate.

An entire army was intent on survival, so
Refugees were spurned.
Civilians were trampled underfoot and their
Farm carts overturned.

Vehicles were running on wheel rims,
Others rearing out of control,
And obstructive refugees were murdered,
All part of the inevitable toll.

Eventually, as the military exodus dwindled,
And the roads began to clear,
The refugees resumed their long trek south,
Kim's family close to the rear.

In silent anguish they slogged along,
Flotsam floating in the night,
With no idea of where they were heading:
Peasants in despairing flight.

Then the Chinese shelled without warning,
Part of a ruthless ploy,
To scatter the refugees for ever, allowing
Their troops to deploy.

They went to their deaths in thousands,
Scythed down at a stroke,
And among those who weren't slaughtered
Morale inevitably broke.

All over the rocky peninsular, on hilly paths
And mountain tracks,
Stragglers meandered wearily, worldly goods
Straining bent backs.

When driven to despair by hunger,
They sought a nearby village
But every last one was deserted,
Ghost hamlets due to pillage.

Houses were burned, razed to the ground,
Dead scarred by mutilation,
Wanton slaughter by North Korean fiends
Not armies in confrontation.

Then the first signs of UN resistance
Gradually began to appear.
Artillery rumbled amid distant hills and
Mortars coughed at the rear.

Eventually came their final lap, and with
The help of an ebony night
They slithered through the Chinese lines,
And into the promised light.

As dawn broke they reached their haven,
So happy and elated
That they spun their story with alacrity,
Expecting to be fêted.

But a colonel, viewing them with an evil eye,
Led them to a lonesome spot,
Where he lined them up in due military style
And promptly had them shot.

The atrocity went unrecorded, a triviality
That happened all the time,
And because Kim cringed behind his father
He alone survived the crime.

He froze in silence beneath dead bodies,
Soaked in his father's gore,
And when all became still again, he fled,
Scared witless to the core.

He hadn't the faintest idea of what to do
Or where to turn for aid,
And after days of aimless wandering
All hopes began to fade.

His worst problem was the pain of hunger,
With rarely a morsel to eat,
And as he foraged around for victuals came
The ugliest face of defeat.

Not pole-axed or menaced by the armies
Locked in bloody affray,
But beaten and kicked by locals, bent on
Keeping strangers at bay.

So Kim was utterly forsaken, no one giving
A damn for his plight,
But his instinct for survival enabled him to
Buck the odds and fight.

In Seoul he joined a gang of street urchins,
Young thugs without a care,
And they taught Kim how to pick pockets,
Spurred on by natural flair.

Then came a purge by the police, forcing
Them all to disperse,
To flee into the country where conditions
Had never been worse.

So, as days passed and the seasons changed,
Kim re-trod the war-torn land;
And as his fortunes reached their lowest ebb
He chanced on a military band.

It was the Dukes proudly marching off to war
With locals flocking all around,
Cheering us on as we headed for the Samichon:
Our first taste of hostile ground.

12 Platoon was stationed well to the rear,
With Animal Evans at the end,
And when a flagging Kim grasped his hand,
He immediately found a friend.

They marched on in tandem, then Kim was
Hoisted on to Animal's pack
And by the time we reached our destination,
No way was Kim going back.

Thus, by accident, we acquired a houseboy
Whose presence was a delight,
And though he wore our badge and uniform
He was never allowed to fight.

The Samichon River position (Yong Dong) was regarded as a soft area in which new units could acclimatize themselves. In our case, this turned out to be a fallacy. Rupert describes his first glimpse of no man's land and he refers to the vexed question of patrolling and the domination of no man's land. At one stage, with ambitious company commanders trying to impress their superiors, the whole thing got so out of hand, with scores of unnecessary casualties, that the divisional commander (Major General M.M. A-R-West) issued a directive that no patrols were to be sent out without a justifiable objective in view.

No Man's Land

No man's land! A paddy jungle where men lurk
Like rabid canine strays,
Taking advantage of murky darkness in order
To weave their evil ways.

I wait for dawn, anxious to appraise this
Eerie, inscrutable, divide:
A killing-ground where shifting shadows drift
And human hunters hide.

But as the light of day edges over the hills
I sense only morning calm,
With an opaque mist wafting down the valley,
A veil of beauty and charm.

Bald hills protrude through the damp haze,
Resembling scattered isles,
Each one deep-scarred by twisting trenches
Snaking coastward for miles.

Soon, we too will be tracking and stalking
Over this venomous land
For Earl Gray has decreed nightly patrols
To secure the upper hand.

Patrolling soon got under way and things took a very unusual turn. On our first venture into no man's land we got lost and were unable to locate the narrow path leading back through our barbed wire and minefield. When daylight came we were still milling about the valley. The Chinese soon spotted us and shelled us heavily before we found our way in.

Two nights later we discovered that the Chinese had placed a cloth marker at the entrance of what had previously been our concealed path. Realising the significance of this, we mounted an ambush halfway up the path rather than in no man' s land. That way, any raiding party would be more restricted, trailing along in single file, sandwiched by minefields.

Ambush

Behold, the enemy! Each one squat and thick-set,
An eerie and harrowing sight,
Padding softly, alert and eager, unsuspecting of
An ambush masked by night.

My nerves are taut, my mind agog, dreading
The havoc that lies ahead.
That my short life should come to this: a killer,
About to shoot men dead!

As ordered, we delay our initial fire, waiting
For the whites of their eyes.
Then comes the command to use rapid bursts
To ensure every bastard dies.

Bullets belch forth and we shout and scream,
Exacerbating the confusion,
And with spitting Stens and thudding Brens
There is but one conclusion.

Then I see a Burp gun levelled in my direction
So I pepper him head to chest,
Dramatically he staggers, teeters, twists and turns,
And bleeds towards eternal rest.

Some survive and to a man stampede into the
Minefield rather than succumb,
And as they rampage through darkness we hear
Them blown to kingdom come.

When all is still I relapse into shock:
A reaction that is rife.
Bodies, bodies, littered everywhere,
But not a spark of life.

Oh dear God! Did we really do that?
Oh yes … Oh yes …

After a month we moved to a position opposite the notorious Chinese hill code-named The Boot. Here, we came under frequent shelling which took a steady toll in casualties. For the first time we saw how men reacted when wounded and we went through the agonising procedure of learning how to handle the death of friends.

A Blighty Touch!

The shells cascade down, sudden and unexpected.
Men caught in the open, exposed and unprotected.
One is hit and as his mates rush to render first aid,
Up goes the consoling cry, the one always made.
You're reet, lad. A Blighty touch!'

A mendacious cry to hide the wound's gravity,
A deliberate lie however portentous the cavity.
A lie always welcomed and implicitly believed
The truth simply too appalling to be perceived.
Luck at last, a Blighty touch!

No pain, no feelings: nerves temporarily shattered.
A smile serene, as though nothing else mattered,
Convinced by their promises that he is safe and sound,
He's overcome by joy, knowing he's homeward-bound.
Thank God for a Blighty touch!

When frantic shouts for stretcher-bearers ring out
They bring comfort and reassurance, never doubt.
Then drowsiness clouds his visions of hospitalisation:
Fading images of nurses, clean sheets, and relaxation.
All the joys of a Blighty touch!

Pain surges as he is jerked and jolted down the hill,
And odd spasms are succeeded by a macabre chill.
Then, as they near the morgue at the end of the trench,
Darkness descends: life ousted by an ominous stench.

The MO gives him a cursory glance.
Then back to men still with a chance.
So much for a Blighty touch!

We were, as Major Earl Gray often pointed out, a platoon of misfits, but only one man was a real problem: Bill Oglethorpe. He couldn't handle life in the front line. I realised this and twice sent him back to the MO to secure a safer posting; but the MO had traditional views and sent him back with a flea in his ear. What Bill Oglethorpe then did was quite wrong, but it took guts, although not the type of guts his arch enemy, the MO, had in mind!

The cold spell referred to came from Siberia. Temperatures went down to around -40 degrees Fahrenheit and that is cold!

Frostbite

Insidiously it loomed, and insidiously it struck.
A defect of character; a man cursed by bad luck;
A creeping malady; a slow paralysis of morale;
All words of help and sympathy patently banal.

By nature he was a joker who exuded good cheer,
But at the sight of blood, bonhomie turned to fear
And after the ambush, with bodies ripped and torn,
His spirit was crushed, a man vacuous and forlorn.

Soon, he descended into the depths of black isolation,
The slightest sound making him flinch in anticipation.
When shells fell he was the first to ferret for cover,
Cowering and cringing, needing hours to recover.

Surreptitiously we watched his rapid disintegration,
Some with contempt, others with ghoulish fascination.
And when I sent him sick, to request duties at the rear,
The MO refused, deeming guts the panacea of all fear.

But it wasn't guts which finally gained him a reprieve;
It was shifting winds, bringing cold hard to believe.
Blizzards dragged temperatures lower than ever before,
With icy blasts so brutal they numbed us to the core.

The war stalled, but we lurched on through the motions,
And orders for fresh patrols aroused rebellious emotions.
But Bill saw his chance, a crafty dodge to solve his plight:
He went sockless on patrol, challenging Jack Frost to bite.

It was for him a master-stroke, brilliantly expeditious,
Affording his arch enemy no reason to be suspicious;
And when they flew him to Japan to amputate a toe,
Winston was jubilant: 'By 'eck! That's the way to go.' *

** For the rest of the winter Harry Winston--- forever seeking ways of working his ticket--- never wore socks or gloves, but it didn't do him any good. The extreme cold soon passed and instead of frostbite all he got were blisters and chilblains.*

Once the weather abated, life went back to normal. Rupert continued to post his verses on the platoon notice board. Earl Gray found them increasingly tiresome. He tried to persuade me to put a stop to them, but when that failed he retaliated by pinning a burst of Shakespeare on all the platoon notice boards. He quoted part of King Henry V's famous speech about St Crispin's Day. Needless to say, Rupert could not resist hitting back.

St Crispin's Day

'And gentlemen in England now abed
Shall think themselves accursed they were not here
And hold their manhoods cheap whilst any speaks
That fought with us upon St Crispin's day.'

Rupert's response was deemed to be insolent and for the umpteenth time he was docked a week's pay.

Behold!
Yon shimmering dawn doth herald once more
St Crispin's Day.
The day whereon the Bard, through noble Harry,
extolled us on high
To gather proud English wounds,
and then plug-up a hole and die.

Hark Tommy!
With mighty impudence I doth say:

'Stuff St Crispin's Day!'

Those whingeing union bastards now abed
Won't curse they missed St Crispin's Day.
More likely, in some fag-bespattered loco-shed,
They'll convene a meeting to grab more pay.

We were still opposite the Boot when Earl Gray decreed that each platoon was to provide a sniper. He was to establish a "hide" in no man's land and watch for enemy activity through a brand new, highly developed, telescopic sight. Knowing that Rupert thrived on solitude, and the advisability of keeping him in a low profile, I appointed him platoon sniper. For weeks he went off on his lonesome vigil but never achieved any results, unless one counts the following poem.

The Sniper

Now sits a victim within my sights.
He's smiling and relaxed, at leisure;
Sublimely unaware that his frail life
Lies entirely within my pleasure.

He basks in the sun and waffles on,
No doubt regaling his friends and cronies
With the rights and wrongs of army life,
And denouncing all officers as phonies.

What crazy duty demands that I should kill
This man who cannot remotely matter?
If I shoot the poor sod, what comfort in that?
To see his skull implode, then shatter?

So it's safety catch on and rifle to rest,
My softness acknowledged by a profanity.
Yet inwardly I rejoice, with peace of mind,
Thankful to have retained my humanity.

'Motivation' highlights a problem we all faced-- the need for privacy. If men weren't being disturbed by a mate or Chinese shelling, they could always rely on Old Origins to stick his oar in. Rupert craved privacy in order to compose his poems out loud, and to this end he was often reduced to muttering to himself whilst using one of the latrines. The comment he makes in 'Motivation' about "free of stench" refers to the fact that the hills in the front line had been fought over several times and human remains were never far beneath the surface, giving a distinctive odour of varying intensity.

Motivation

Seeking privacy, I wandered along the lateral trench
And chanced upon a spot pleasantly free of stench.
An ideal haven, away from the madding crowd,
To meditate a mo, before composing out loud:

"I often wonder what inspires our Tommy most?
What crosses his mind when he hears Last Post?
And what does he feel when he fights for others?
Certainly not the fear of joining dead brothers."

Thus, as I cogitated, hoping for divine inspiration,
Old Origins hove-to, wrecking my concentration.

"Laddie! Stop buggering about with that pen and paper.
Get back to your bunker. And I will deal with you later!
I know why the buggers are so vicious and bold:
It's 'cause I've taught 'em to do as they're told!"

I scurried down the trench, put to flight.
Come to think of it, he's probably right.

Wake Up to Reality tells the story of a good friend of Rupert's: Peter Macey. Macey was illiterate and only ever received letters from his elder brother--- a drunkard, a cynic, and a communist fellow-traveller who was a shop steward at the liquorice factory in Pontefract. Macey always got Rupert to read these letters to him and they were nothing but tirades, castigating Macey for fighting on the wrong side. When Macey died, Rupert threatened to write to his brother and tell him a few home truths; but he never did. Instead I wrote to him explaining that Macey had died bravely. Rupert contented himself with another poem.

Wake Up to Reality

Don't you ever grieve that your countrymen are dying?
Aren't you sickened as they perish in an senseless war?
Don't you ever wake at night and hear troops crying?
Can't you grasp that our enemies are rotten to the core?
Don't you ever see the need for political morality?
Can't you understand how evil these men are?
Won't you ever have the guts to face up to reality,
Instead of getting plastered in a Pontefract bar?

No?

Well, here's news that will put you to the test.
Last night as you staggered home, belching and sighing,
Your young brother lay in a trench, bleeding and dying,
A bullet hole drilled straight through his chest.

Then came a 'Blue-on-Blue' incident. We were shelled by one of our Centurion tanks due to a fresh crew being badly briefed. Our casualties were light (two killed and three wounded), confined to the only section visible to the tank's crew. In all, the shelling went on for an hour. Rupert did sterling work over the field telephone and the 88 wireless set. At first he had great difficulty in convincing Early Gray that we were suffering a Blue-on-Blue, but eventually he succeeded by the strength of his harangueing. Earl Gray was then able to bring it to an end.

Blue-on-Blue

Each dawn bursts forth like a liberating reprieve:
Darkness dissolves, leaving no cloak to deceive.
A time to unwind, to eat, sleep, relax and rest,
Maybe just mooch around, free of any behest.

But we are well aware of the danger of surprise,
And stand ready for any disasters that can arise,
Our vigilance based on a dawn we'll forever rue
When we suffered the tragedy of a Blue-on-Blue.

High on a flanking hill, and diagonally to our rear,
Came a new Centurion, its briefing none too clear;
And at break of day, when they spied us on our hill,
They mistook us for the enemy and lusted for a kill.

Shortly, 20-pounders were hurtling in our direction,
Methodically flattening bunkers in our rear section.
Timbers were torn asunder, strewn across the slope,
Leaving the seven occupants with very little hope.

Then, rising above the cacophony of bursting shells
Came despairing cries and a chorus of piteous yells.
Old Origins acting instinctively, and without delay,
Grabbed a nearby stretcher, ready to enter the fray.

He and a volunteer waited for the next muzzle flash
And when the shell landed, made a suicidal dash.
Bullets from a machine gun chased them all the way,
With the yowling and screaming of many a ricochet.

By sheer good luck, they survived and on their return
Dumped their load and sped back without concern.
They defied all the odds, and ran the gauntlet thrice,
But within feet of safety came a sickening price.

Eventually an enquiry was called to apportion blame.
But 'accidental' was decreed, with no guilt or shame!
A predictable whitewash which we will forever deplore
With a deliberate snub for the noblest act we ever saw.

During this Blue-on-Blue incident I was caught by the blast of a 20-pounder on our last 'home run'. I bled like a pig (as one does with head wounds), but in the end my injuries amounted to nothing worse than split ear-drums and total (but temporary) deafness. A helicopter evacuated me to an American Mash Unit and eventually I was sent back to the British Commonwealth Hospital in Kure. Once recovered I was given a soft posting in the local headquarters. I wrote to Rupert several times, telling him what a great time I was having, especially my discovery of sex with a lovely Japanese girl. At the time I had no idea that 12 Platoon was having a really tough time on Hill 355. Nor that they had fallen out in a big way with their new platoon commander named Staples. He forbade Rupert to post verses on the notice board and he even tried (unsuccessfully) to get members of the platoon to report to him whenever Rupert spread new verses around by hand. The only poem that survives from this period was one sent to me in Japan.

Beware!

We Tommies at the front suffer, sir,
We Tommies in our trenches die,
And all in the name of freedom, sir,
Though few of us understand why.
Yet officers like you abound, sir.
Fornicating and skiving at the rear.
Forever wine women and song, sir,
With nowt but the clap to fear.
But your cushy job is an illusion, sir.
In the end war always wins.
Notice the cross-bones of death, sir,
And the skull above it that grins.

The Bloody Hook

A few weeks later Rupert's prophecy came true. Earl Gray spent his R and R in Kure and when he saw my luxurious life-style he was so incensed that he had me posted back to Korea. Lieutenant Staples was given a cushy job as Signals Officer and I resumed command of 12 Platoon. Soon afterwards, we relieved the Black Watch on The Hook.

The Hook was a steep-sided, crescent-shaped ridge that dominated the countryside for miles around. It was like the hinges of a door. On its left flank the UN line plunged to the south west and if the hinges went, and the door flew open, the UN line to the east would be ripe for a traditional roll-up operation, leaving Seoul totally exposed.

The Hook was so vital that more men died on it than any other hill in Korea. It had become a fortress: totally bare through so much shelling with a sophisticated network of trenches, tunnels, and fighting bunkers. Orders on the Hook were straightforward: hold to the last man.

Taking Up the Challenge

Now dawns the day we'll never forget,
Dawns the day we will forever regret,
When came our turn to bear the brunt
And defend The Hook on the UN front.
The sharpest end of freedom.

Ahead of us dust spirals in the air,
Ahead of us a hill blown totally bare,
Where shot and shell rage all night:
Continuous mayhem, a pitiless fight.
The struggle for freedom.

Marching undaunted, refusing to be shaken,
Marching to a hill that must never be taken.
No option but to fight, to see the battle through.
No retreat, no relief: no escaping a bloody do.
We'll fight like tigers for freedom.

Halfway up, evidence of battle littered around,
Halfway up, recent dead piled high in a mound.
Silence engulfs us and our complexions pale:
The odour of death, so debilitating to inhale.
Men killed in the cause of freedom.

We plod along in silence, ever upwards;
Plod to the summit, facing northwards,
Relieving exhausted and depleted Jocks,
Men who've stood firm, steady as rocks.
Men who've given their all for freedom.

We take over bunkers, deep and musty.
Take over Brownings, worn but trusty.
Weapons that swing and arc at will,
All rates on rapid for maximum kill.
The art of defending freedom.

We recoil at a hill in such a cadaverous state.
Recoil at rats, strutting with an arrogant gait.
Mammoth rats, human flesh so nourishing;
Detested rats, numbers forever flourishing.
The horror of defending freedom.

Foul views of Chinese dead decorating our wire,
And foul bunkers with over-lapping fields of fire.
Bunkers so weakened by persistent shelling
That how long they'll last, there is no telling.
        The risk of defending freedom.

Tension increases as every man is assigned a task,
A tension exacerbated by the risks they unmask,
And every man jack fears that this will be
The last place on earth he will ever see.
        The end of our freedom?

He looked over the trench and stared ahead;
Looked in curiosity and exposed his head,
Absorbing the details of each Chinese hill,
All dusty and misshapen, suspiciously still.
        Too innocent to threaten freedom?

No warning! No sound! One clean strike!
No second chance. Just one dead Tyke.
He paid the price for being reckless
Now he lies there, damn near headless.
        Dead in the cause of freedom!

A Lost Friend

Today I lost a good friend,
A loss time will never mend.
He was only nineteen,
Tall, hungry, and lean,
But a bullet went straight through his brain.

Today I lost a good friend.
A lad who would never offend.
So blushing and shy
He had no right to die,
But a bullet still went straight through his brain.

Today I lost a good friend
Who once went on a bend.
And tanked up on beer
He boasted of no fear,
But that damn bullet went straight through his brain.

Today I lost a good friend
Who loved his girl no end.
Far too besotted ever to stray
He lived only for their big day,
Then that fucking bullet went straight through his brain.

Men in 12 platoon rarely questioned why they were fighting in Korea. They found the subject sterile. As men in the Great War used to say, 'We're here because we're here.' Rupert was not so easily satisfied and he tried to analyse the situation. His comparison with Shakespeare's 'band of brothers' is like an echo coming down the ages. This spirit of brotherhood, of unity and camaraderie, seems to grips all fighting men in desperate situations, whether at Rorke's Drift, The Alamo, Dunkirk, Dien Bien Phu, or Stalingrad.

The Reason Why

When bugles out of darkness sound,
Then battle will commence;
And flying metal in the round
May well despatch us hence.
Waves of Chinese will emerge,
Hordes in awesome spate,
Howling zombies on the surge,
Inspired by political hate.
Leaping our wire, forever firing,
Pushing forward mighty fast,
Sprinting upwards, never tiring,
Until shot or caught by blast.

So it will be, with the Duke's at the ready.
Every bunker manned, every man steady!
Yet if disaster strikes and we should die
Is there, remotely, any good reason why?

So often is heard that tiresome query,
Always answered by the same old theory,
That in the cause of freedom we will die.
What cock! What a hollow, mocking lie.
And it's just the same with abstract aspirations:
What's gained by dying for the United Nations?
Fifty years hence, what chance they'll see us right?
What politician will give a damn for our plight?
Their glib promises are nothing but propaganda,
So here's the plain truth told with utter candour.

Together in combat we have felt death's claw;
Retched in disgust at the sight of human gore
Draining from pals who've died on a foreign field
For a corrupt cause to which no man should yield.
We've lived as rats, heard men cry out for their mothers,
And in our anguish become another a band of brothers.
So yes, we will fight! Slug it out until the battle ends,
But for no other reason than to safeguard our friends.

Occasionally, there were quiet nights on The Hook, but by day the shelling and mortaring never stopped. It made proper sleep impossible. Several men came close to cracking under the strain. Before long the danger of men falling asleep while on stag duty became so acute that they were relieved every hour. Only one man was ever found fast asleep at his post, but I was well aware that many men had to fight hard not to nod off, if only momentarily. I only realised Rupert was one of those who succumbed to tiredness when I read the following poem.*

Nodding Off

As stars hang high and the moon drifts
Regally over a peaceful night,
I scan the scarred hills that spread like
Fingers, feeling left and right.

I marvel at such unfamiliar stillness,
The eerie calm of a hiatus,
And I relax, sensing that for a change
Bedlam won't overtake us.

Soon, flickering flares cast ebbing shadows
Over the mouldering terrain,
And sepia tints blur the fading hills flanking
The Samichon's placid plain.

Then out of the gloom vague figures appear,
Our lines their destination:
Ghosts gliding through our tangled barbed wire
Without care or hesitation.

Soon I see them sharp and clear, their auras
Too solid for an aberration,
With their blood-stained uniforms revealing
Their theatres of operation.

The Old Contemptibles, the Desert Rats,
14th Army, and Red Coats too,
Straight from the raw mayhem of Mons,
Tobruk, Imphal, and Waterloo.

They come to see us tread a battlefield
Such as our forefathers trod,
Knowing many will share their fate and
Rot beneath the foreign sod.

They see us as fresh cannon-fodder who,
Having fought with luck galore
And endured the demise of many a mate,
Now quake before death's door.

Then my phantoms fade: the spell is broken.
My head jerks back; jaded eyes flash open.
I succumb to panic, to guilt and contrition,
Ashamed at having imperilled our position.

* *The man found asleep on stag (on three different occasions) was a sixteen year-old Katcom. Being a persistent offender, and unable to understand a word of English, two ROK liaison officers were called in to sort matters out. Whilst most of us slept, recovering from a hard night on patrols, the lad was taken into a nearby re-entrant and made to dig a grave. He was then shot in the back of the head. The liaison officers then left without a word to anyone. When furious protests were made all that happened was that the liaison officers were posted to another sector. In some ways it was our worst experience in Korea. Full details are recorded in The Bloody Hook.*

One thing we all loathed about The Hook were the dead Chinese left dangling on our barbed wire. Their numbers increased with every attack. It was far too dangerous to remove them and although men often tried to shoot them out of the vertical, or blast them clear with grenades, it seldom worked.

It is interesting to note that 'Hanging on The Old Barbed Wire' was the title of a popular song in the Great War. I don't know if Rupert was aware of this.

Hanging On The Old Barbed Wire

Oh how I wish you festering stiffs
Would miraculously go away.
God rot your gaseous guts and make
Your flesh wither and decay.
May rain and shine lambaste you
Into early deterioration,
And a hell-bound wind whisk your remains
Into eternal damnation.

But there you repose, you poor rotting sods,
Mocking us the livelong day,
Your faces peeling down to skulls, tongues
Lolling limply as if to say:
'Come hither friends. Here it all ends.
Come share our merciful fate.
Death alone brings peace and harmony;
No more lies or political hate.'

So there you dangle, having forfeited
Your lives in the call of duty.
By communist lights, noble gestures,
To commissars, acts of beauty.
But we see you in a different light:
A vision of how we may expire.
Fetid meat and bloated feet,
Hanging on the old barbed wire.

Rupert's great friend, Harry Winston, had a theory that it was safer to dodge shells in an open trench than take cover in a bunker. He believed that shells, like lightning, never struck the same place twice. It was nonsense, of course, but he had the luck of the devil and laughed with delight at numerous narrow escapes. Ironically, it was only after Corporal Holroyd had ordered him to take cover in a bunker that he met his end. The bunker received two direct hits in quick succession and collapsed. By the time we dug him out, he had suffocated.

Poor Simple Sod!

Oh, you poor simple sod!
For you above all, I have harboured fears.
And for you alone I'll spill inconsolable tears.
And even though the fate of all the others is galling,
At least they understood the dangers of their calling;
But never in our nation's most pressing needs
Should you have faced such deadly deeds.
A dullard, not even able to read or write,
Daft as a brush but made to fight.
Oh, you poor simple sod!

The biggest blow to our morale was a new type of Chinese mine, one which they often placed on our patrol routes. Unlike other mines, it did not explode when weight was put on it. At that point there was a loud 'clonk!' but it only detonated when the weight was removed. Men were known to remain stationery on these mines in abject terror for minutes on end, knowing that once the 'clonk' had been heard there was no escape. If others went to their aid, they would only be blown up as well.

Foul Weapon

Death is constantly with us, come what may,
Striking us down without mercy, day on day.
Sometimes it's a sniper with a single stroke,
At other times shells, amid billowing smoke.

We do our best to stop our fears from showing
And seldom dwell on the manner of our going,
But our major dread has become a new creation,
A mine purpose-built for personal obliteration.

Designed by psychopaths with evil imagination,
It has a pause between priming and detonation.
A plunger warns of what is about to take place:
Gives time to ponder, then kills without trace.

Old Origins was the first victim of this foul device
And even when snared offered us typical advice.
He ordered us to scatter and watch him leap clear:
We obeyed and saw him atomised, then disappear.

An old soldier who never died
But was simply blown away.

After we had been on The Hook three weeks, air reconnaissance reported Chinese forces assembling in vast numbers. At the same time there was a noticeable surge in Chinese shelling. Stretching back to divisional HQ, Brass Hats became increasingly anxious about the outcome of the coming battle. Fresh orders were issued daily on how to hold the hill. They did nothing to boost our morale. In truth, a month was too long on The Hook in those conditions; but that was the system, and army systems were sacrosanct. Also, Earl Gray would have died of shame if we had been pulled off early. Not surprisingly, what little grumbling there was about this was aimed at the Brass Hats - who else?

The Agony of Waiting ...

Orders spew forth and are duly ignored:
The same old gubbins.
The Brass Hats after glory, the price paid
By poor old Muggins.

Shelling keeps the Brass rooted to the rear,
A truancy hardly inspiring
For it is at their behest we are urged to be
Ever vigilant and untiring.

Yet how much longer can we hold on with our
Casualties mounting?
Pride demands that we feign indifference, but
Everyone's counting.

And as the stretcher-bearers shuttle past
In a continuous procession
The gnawing hunger for a Blighty touch
Balloons into an obsession.

Stand-to! Oh, how we loathe it as the sun
Takes its time to sink,
Leaving us poised, weapons cocked, with
Nowt to do but think.

We stare across the barren, disfigured hills
Imagining divers fates,
Mostly the void of eternal darkness that
Death alone activates.

So we revert to fond images of home
And domestic banality:
Parents, girl-friends, drinking mates,
And childhood triviality.

Then as the sun slips below the hills, night
Descends like a curtain:
Now is the moment! Now one thing will
Test us out for certain.

With the echoing boom of thunder
The milk round arrives.
Such vicious shelling it's a miracle
That anyone survives.

It's always the same, as they pound us
Night after night,
With great orange fireballs sparking
Darkness alight.

Down they crunch, each belabouring
Us like a hammer.
No let up, no respite, no mercy:
Constant clamour.

Earth churning and spewing, often
Exhuming the dead,
The darkness buzzing and hissing
With white-hot lead.

Then the milk-round fizzles and silence
Descends: all is still.
We strain for the sound of bugles that
Herald the final kill.

Waiting! Waiting! The tense hours leave
Our tangled nerves twitching,
With dank palms and weapons raised,
Coiled trigger-fingers itching.

Another hour and our eyes ache from
Scanning the wire,
Then another hour of shifting shapes,
Tempting us to fire.

And as these eerie shadows move,
Inching up the slopes,
A mist swirls and twists, forever
Diminishing our hopes.

Deep into the night we are still standing-to,
The Chinese are yet to come.
Another Rubicon evaded, so we celebrate
With prodigious tots of rum.

The night passes in an alcoholic haze as
Peace rules the terrain.
Then on to another day, the same bloody
Waiting all over again.

Eventually we captured a prisoner. He said the attack would come on the night of May 28th two days before we were to be relieved. He also claimed that if the attack was successful it would herald a full-scale offensive aimed at recapturing Seoul.

This gave rise to frantic activity. We had no time to mope over what was now certain to happen. However, on the morning of May 28th Rupert pinned a poem on the notice board. It was so mournful that I would normally have removed it, but in this case Fletcher got to it first and added a line which gave everyone such a good laugh that it did morale a power of good.

May 28th 1953

Now dawns a day of awesome fear,
A day of death for which we are fated,
With orders repeated, crisp and clear:
To the last man, or enemy annihilated.

The great unknown descends tonight,
Bringing days of torment to their end.
Our destiny settled in a climactic fight
On which the lives of so many depend.

It's the ultimate test a man can face,
That culminates with God disposing:
Miraculously spared by His grace
Or else scattered wide, decomposing.

God help us all,
God save us all,
Especially those deserving.

"That's cooked my goose then, you bastard." Fletch.

The battle duly came. For a time we held them off with small arms fire, but eventually sheer numbers overwhelmed us and they spilled into our trenches. I gave the order to retire to our tunnels. There, we spent the rest of the night fighting them off at the entrances, leaving the Gunners to scythe them down with air-burst shells. The UN artillery fired 38,000 rounds that night: the Chinese probably a few thousand short of that, giving a total of well over 50,000. Think about it! Fifty thousand shells on a hill not much bigger than Haytor. No one in Korea had ever experienced anything like it.

In the morning, just ten of my platoon were able to walk off the hill. Of the old hands, only Corporal Holroyd, Fletcher, and I escaped unscathed. Rupert had been wounded. Holroyd and I carried him down the hill to the CAP. His wound was relatively minor--- a flesh wound on his right thigh--- and I was confident he would survive.

Later that day, after we had dug out those buried alive, the Royal Fusiliers relieved us. The following morning I went to visit Rupert in an American MASH unit. He had died two hours before I arrived. During the night he had scribbled a note for me which he left with a nurse: his last poem.

Tell 'Em

Tell 'em Saj! Let your ink
Gush and flow bright red.
How it really was: our fears,
And how freely we bled.

No poetic fantasies, please:
No symbolic flights of a dove,
Just how we held the Hook,
Sharing pride and agarpy love.*

** Rupert misspelt 'agarpy', no doubt for my benefit. Really, it is agape (pronounced 'agarpy') but Rupert knew I would not be familiar with it. As I eventually discovered, it is Greek, meaning ultimate, non-physical, love.*

Epilogue

Over fifty years have passed since all that happened. I followed Rupert's wishes and wrote about our experiences on The Hook. In fact, in the intervening years I have written four novels about the Korean War. Rupert's poems have never aroused any interest among publishers. Consequently, I am now financing them myself. There is nothing new about that with poetry, but it does at least give me the right to add two poems of my own, albeit in Rupert's style.

The bugler in 'Last Post' was Ron Jenkins. He was desperately anxious about his close mate Joe Boothroyd, thought to be buried in the forward tunnel. It was a mission into the unknown since Chinese working parties were clearing away their dead in the valleys, but no shots were exchanged.*

* *Joe Boothroyd was among those saved. On being dug out, he asked: 'Who won?'*

Last Post

Later, he volunteered to help dig out the entombed,
Among them, his mate.
But the hill was in such a shambolic state that most
Rescues came too late.

Trenches were flattened and wiring laid to waste, with
Timbers strewn around,
And piles of butchered bodies confirmed the depravity
Of a spent battleground.

By chance his bugle was found amid the ruins, so he
Put it to his lips and blew,
And although it was twisted, dented, and crumpled,
Notes came, clear and true.

He got permission to break off from those digging,
Determined to honour them all,
And he strode to The Hook's peak spurning danger,
Then prepared to sound his call.

His silhouette was etched against the skyline,
Ramrod, as if on parade,
And amid the desolation his statuesque figure
Was a sight never to fade.

His poignant tune was so fluent and haunting
That he invoked the Holy Ghost
And those who bore witness watched in wonder
As the dead absorbed Last Post.

I wrote 'Photo on the Wall' some years later. When I moved to Tenerife I hung the photograph directly above my desk. I looked at it so often that eventually I felt compelled to write about it. It is still there, even as I write this on January 10th 2008. The same photograph also forms the front cover of this book. Those who survived The Hook will no doubt recognise themselves. Rupert Sandwitch took the photograph with my Kodak Baby Brownie.

Photo on the Wall

Framed photo hanging on my study wall,
Images of times perchance best forgotten?
Oh, no! This sepia-dappled record of the past,
Lacking focus and generally misbegotten,
Depicts the young lads of my old platoon,
Lads who, amid a storm of flying metal, I led
On The Hook, a Korean hill of foulest carnage
Where all but ten foundered and finished dead.
Young conscripts - Teddy Boys - rascals all,
Who only now, after years of lingering reflections,
I've grown to know, love, and even understand.
Such normal lads, so enhanced by imperfections,
But disciplined soldiers for all their faults
With Yorkshire grit, most cussed to be found;
Not swayed by hopes of medals or vain glory,
Just Tommies, determined to hold their ground.
When they died, many tearful farewells were bid
But who cares now what those faded images did?

None, save I.

They died for strangers on a foreign hill.
They lie there still.

Dead Dukes

they are now, my boys,

So that concludes their story.

Tommy Atkins

lives for ever, my boys,

So did they

enhance his glory?

Glossary

Katcoms:	Korean soldiers attached to British units.
ORs:	Other Ranks.
CP:	Command Post.
Morgue:	Company Aid Post (CAP).
Bren:	Light machine gun with bipod.
Sten:	Hand-held light machine gun.
Burp gun:	Chinese hand-held machine gun.
Jankers:	Type of army punishment.
ROK:	Republic of Korea (South)
R and R:	Rest and Recuperation (leave)
Blighty:	Britain (home)
HQBCFK:	Headquarters British Commonwealth Forces in Korea.
Stand-to:	Ready for action in trenches.
Stand-down:	Return to normal.
Milk Round:	An artillery bombardment that arrives regularly, without fail.
MSR:	Main Supply Route
Medicine and duty:	'No sympathy. Nothing wrong with you!'
Snout:	Tobacco
2 i/c:	Second-in-command
Blue-on-Blue:	Hit by 'friendly' fire

ACCLAIM FOR

'THE WAR POEMS OF A YOUNG SOLDIER'

"I read these poems with a feeling of awe. They are unique and harrowing ... Brilliant!"

Sir Christopher Ondaatje.

"Rarely has a collection of poems so captured the horror, tragedy, humour, and pathos of war."

'The Morning Calm'

"He (Hollands) clearly is passionate about what he wants to say; outspoken about the trial and awfulness of war; and reflective on the life of soldiers in and out of battle ... A very loyal Duke."

'The Iron Duke'

"I found myself reading the book, putting it down, and then being drawn back to it, either to read another poem or re-read one I had just finished. The book will hold a special place in my library."

Michael Kirk (brother of 1st Bn I DWR Subaltern)

"I've read the book from cover to cover three times, endeavouring to find a favourite poem. Quite pointless. I like them all. They're great. The watercolours were an inspired inclusion."

David Gascoyne, (1st Bn DWR, Subaltern)

"Hollands is no Kipling but, as with Owen and Sassoon, his poems will be read for as long as wars continue ... I marvel at the heart-felt outpourings of a 19 year-old national serviceman."

Edward Gaskell (Publisher)

"These poems are more telling and revealing of National Service than anything else I have ever read."

Rev A J Bowyers, Ex-Army Chaplain, Korea.

"These poems will live for ever."

Major Alan Fradgley RE MBE

"No war has ever been so brilliantly chronicled by a single poet ... These poems capture the essence and horror of Korea and are incredibly perceptive of human nature."

Paul Willey Ex-BBC Editor.

"This collection of poems is a great example of Hollands's versatility as a writer."

Trevor Hunt, Author of *Ibiza Shorts*.

"When you contrast the smiling young faces on the cover to the stark hell of the poems inside, you get the true spirit of Tommy Atkins."

Guy Bellamy, Author of *Secret Lemonade Drinker*.

"At last we have a highly evocative record of Korea ... What it was like for the rank and file ... These poems should be compulsory reading for all politicians."

Mike Sampson, Author/Historian

In 1956, on the publication of
***The Dead, the Dying and the Damned*,**
Nancy Spain of the *Daily Express* wrote:

"Only when a genius like Hollands
writes the truth about war
will the miracle come
when it will be
no more."